Small bits of horror

AF632808

Tony Myers

BookLeaf Publishing

Presentation by *BookLeaf Publishing*

Web: www.bookleafpub.com

E-mail: info@bookleafpub.com

ISBN : 9789357699327

First edition 2022

PREFACE

I see this book as something experimental, something I did as a challenge and to try new themes and perspectives.
I don't want to sound pretentious and say "It's an experimental art piece" but it's an experimental art piece.
Enjoy!

A Horror Haiku

I have had a thought,
To write a horror haiku,
I'm not good at it.

The Last Man

Papers, research lay upon a table,
Hope had sprouted,
Come to end a horrific fable.

A scientist remained, doctor Xavier,
Toiling away, humanity's savior.
Residing in a bunker, away from them,
The thought of leaving, he could not condemn.

A disease swept the land, unsure of how it
started,
Our doctor works day and night,
To avenge those who have departed.

They shamble, they creek,
They shuffle and groan.
The ones afflicted,
No longer remember home.

Their minds have melted, primal instincts in
control.
Their hunger for human flesh, had taken its toll.

Xavier was close, he knew he could solve it,
But he feared he was too late, he could hear
them.

Pounding.

The doors to his lab, could only take so much,
"Hurry!" He thought, working in a rush.

Bang! Bang! Bang!
The door nearly giving way,
But he could not leave, no, he had to stay.

"I've almost got it, the cure to this disease!"
But he was too late, they broke in with ease.

Wobbling, shaking, crawling and jogging,
They swarmed our scientist,
Consuming his noggin'.

They ate, devoured, munched and crunched,
Filling up on humanity's hero,
All for their lunch.

Streets filled with corpses, littered with carrion,
Hope has left us all,
There's no reason to carry on.

Horror Haiku 2: Electric Boogaloo

Here's another go,
I'm not much of a poet,
But I love haikus.

Howl

Clouds obscured a full moon, thick as the night,
Hiding the moon's presence, blocking its light.
A hunter covers his tracks, not wanting to be followed,
He knew his quarry was near, it's roars in the distance bellowed.

Upon setting the darkness, the sky began to cry,
The rain came down hard, the night no longer dry.

The hunter walked through cobbled streets,
His prey was so much closer,
He could still hear its blood-curdling howls,
Denting his composure.

Silver makes it scream, at least,
That's what he had heard,
But if his bullets didn't do the trick,
He wouldn't be able to spread the word.

The stench of blood stained the cobbles and his nose,
From what the hunter found that night,
A body, half decomposed.

How long had it been there?
He could not be sure.
The night was plagued with evil,
And the hunter was the cure.

Snarling and growling, the beast was near,
It was time for action, no time for fear.
He locked and loaded his pistol with silver,
The hunter felt cold, he began to shiver.

The beast appeared, with teeth aplenty,
It had to die, it's victims ten a penny.

A bullet left the chamber,
Slicing through the air,
The projectile made an impact,
The monster cried in despair.

The creature fell with a thud and a pound,
Its large frame smashed into the ground.
The beast was gone, shot dead in the street,
Sent to hell, after a grisly defeat.

Trapped

I cannot escape,
But I search for the way out,
It will never come.

Gaze

She watches me sleep,
She holds a knife to my throat,
She watches me die.

Chuckle

The clown stood goofy and tall,
His nose was all shiny and red,
Give it a squeeze, you might just laugh,
A clown, with a silly head.

His face was bright and happy,
But something seemed a little off,
Look at him the wrong way,
He may just frown and scoff.

The clown was loved by all,
But you knew there was something wrong,
Every kid's party he attended,
There were one or two children gone.

Where were they going? Nobody knew where they went,
But the clown seemed to know all, he had sinister intent.

He was not a normal clown, Bobby he was named,
Bobby the clown, they called,
Bobby the clown they said.

He knew where those kids were,

He knew why they weren’t in their beds.
He snatched them he did,
In the dead of night, and placed them in his shed.

Chase

I run down a hall,
I can feel it behind me,
It breathes down my neck.

Forgotten

I've been gone so long,
Leaves fall where I am buried,
Here I lie rotting.

Lost

I miss everyone,
I'm from a faraway land,
I cannot return.

Pieces

Did you bring it? Yes! one arm and a leg,
Do we have enough?
No, keep stealing from the dead.

We're building a creature, one man of many,
If we do it right, we could be rich already.
We could master death, loved ones remade,
We could sell out methods, finally, get paid.

But Master is it right? What we're doing
tonight?
Are you questioning me? Here, stitch that arm
on tight.

No Master, I just worry, if its ethical is all,
No, it's not ethical boy, we're making him 8ft
tall.
Have you ever seen a man? Such a mesh of
parts.
Surely it's not right, to mess with those who did
depart.

Boy, I don't know what to tell you,
You keep questioning my commands,
Question me again, and I'll bring out the
reprimands.

Master, I'm sorry, it's just, we've made an awful creation,
One man's arm, a lady's leg, what an abomination.

It's called a creative license, we've made him all our own,
We're borrowing from the dead, now please, don't moan.

Master look! The heart I stole, looks to be beating again,
See dear boy, our science works, life is all the same.

Ah I see, it's raising its hand and placing it around your neck,
Master I'm worried, it feels too tight, please would you come and check?

Is it supposed to be gripping master? It feels awfully tight,
Oh no dear boy, I can't get it off, it's got superhuman might.

Master, I'm choking, get it off quick! I fear I may end up dead.

That's alright boy, it'll all be okay, our creation does need a head.

Vacant

My veins are empty,
Drained from creatures of the night,
Vampires do suck.

Thirst

I thirst for blood, I wish I didn't,
But it tastes so sweet,
And it keeps me efficient.
It gives me the strength to keep on going,
I wish I could stop, but the thirst keeps growing.

I watch and I stalk, I avoid the sun,
If I go out in it, well, it's not much fun.
My pale skin crackles and burns in daylight,
That and crosses, give me a fright.

I must keep drinking, to the last drop,
Maybe I like it, perhaps I'll never stop.

The rush I feel as I sink in my teeth,
It gives me a thrill, to puncture underneath.
I like it when they run, it makes it a challenge,
But they can't escape, as I hunt and I scavenge.

You know what I am, it obvious now,
Why humans you say? Why not drink from a cow.
It's not the same I say, humans are just too sweet.
I'll never stop eating them, they make me complete.

Ouch! I’ve been stabbed! A stake through the
heart!
Why would you do that?
You’ve torn me apart!

I guess now I die, my skin going limp and flat,
I should have flown away, should have turned
into a bat.

Oh well, never mind, I was five hundred years
old,
Perhaps it's for the best if my story is not retold.

Sands

The clock ticks by fast,
Time is something I don't have,
I wish I had more.

Cult

Here we gather,
To see what those who wronged us receive,
Our punishment is swift,
Without mercy or reprieve.

They remain tied to a tree,
That's where heretics go,
Soon it will all be over,
Their damnation would follow.

They beg and they plead,
They know not what they ask,
To let them go now,
Would be a harrowing task.

They'd tell the authorities,
We can't have that,
Once the log comes,
Well, they'd soon go splat.

LOG, LOG, LOG, LOG, LOG,
We chant.
A huge log lined up,
To crush them flat.

They scream and holler,

Begging us to cease,
But we fire the log,
And suddenly, peace.

Awkward

I died long ago, I shamble and I'm awkward,
Back when cats were our gods,
Although that doesn't help much,
Cats are still worshipped today.

I lay wrapped up in bandages,
With all my innards gone.

If you break into my bedroom,
I'll curse those that do.

I know what you're thinking,
This doesn't rhyme,
Well, I've been dead for thousands of years,
English is new to me.

Besides, not all poems rhyme.
It's about expression. Or so I'm told.

I'm a mummy if you couldn't guess.

Murder

Dawn struck down, a corpse lay bare and spread,
Early hours present, a gash carved into the man's head.

Wounded and sliced, with organs missing,
Fluid and gases escaped, leaking and hissing.

Bones broken and flesh swollen like a tyre,
Nobody yet knows, who struck the cadaver.

Laid to waste, along with refuge,
Disposed of like trash, upon a landscape so huge.

As morning rolled in, seagulls came for their meeting,
Gathering around the body, pecking and eating.

Evidence consumed, filling avian bellies,
A man had gone missing, on everyone's tellies.

How could this happen? In a town so pleasant,
Never to be recovered, a murder unpleasant.

Unstoppable

It is on its way,
An entity with a scythe,
It comes for us all.

Puppet

I pull all the strings I do,
Yes, I do, I pull them.
I always get what I want,
Because I'm the puppet demon.

I see your life, I watch and wait,
I see you manage your things,
If you have what I want,
It's time to pull my strings.

You climb the stairs, I might make you trip,
It depends if I want it.
You can't see me, I'm invisible to you,
Unless I shall permit.

Sleep well tonight, I think I'll let you,
I'm in control of everything,
But if I get bored, I'll wake you up,
And I'll cut your bedsprings.

I sit on the end of your bed, while you sleep,
I follow you to work,
You're my puppet, I'm the master,
Oh, this makes me smirk.

Do your job, and I'll do mine,

What a joyous arrangement,
But don't do as I please and you will see,
I'll show you my derangement.

Visitors

Flying high up in the sky,
Just out of your view.
If we fancy, we might just land,
Perhaps we'll abduct you.

We'll take you up into the stars,
Show you the infinite abyss,
But if we decide, your time is up,
We're sure you won't be missed.

We might bring you back,
It depends on a few factors.
If we find you useful,
We won't throw you in the trash compactor.

So let us experiment, put a probe where we shouldn't,
It's fine, we're not from this world,
But try and fight us, disobey or sleight us,
And well, your life will unfurl.
Out of the airlock…

End

Experimental,
I'd say these poems have been,
I think they've been fun.

www.ingramcontent.com/pod-product-compliance
Lightning Source LLC
Chambersburg PA
CBHW051752130826
49812CB00033B/1121